TABLE OF CONTENTS

INTRODUCTION:

IS THIS BOOK FOR YOU?

If you want to be successful in your chosen profession, this book is for you.

If you want to generate substantial revenue streams, this book is for you.

If you want to meet someone loving and compatible, and finally have a successful, enduring relationship, this book is for you.

If you want to lose weight effectively and effortlessly, maintain your ideal weight, and become physically fit, this book is for you.

If you want to heal yourself and maximize your longevity and well-being, this book is for you.

If you want to become emotionally stable and happy, in control of your thoughts and emotions, rather than being controlled and victimized by them, this book is for you.

If you want to reach elevated spiritual planes, this book is for you.

If you want to help heal and transform the planet, end wars and famine, and create peace on Earth, this book is for you.

If you've tried a variety of talk therapies to help you gain insight and change your mind and your world, and yet you still don't have the life that you want, this book is for you.

If you've tried a variety of alternative therapies such as meditation, chanting, affirmations, creative visualizations, and yoga, among others, and yet inner peace and contentment are still beyond your grasp, this book is for you.

If you've attended numerous seminars, conferences and workshops and yet you're still attending seminars, conferences and workshops, this book is for you.

If you've read <u>The Secret</u>, a brilliant and powerful book, but you haven't yet attracted everything you want from the universe, and you're still not happy with your life, this book is for you.

If you've read <u>The Power Of Now</u>, an equally brilliant work of enlightenment and truth, but you're not yet living in the Now, still stuck in the past or the future, still stuck in guilt, shame and fear, this book is for you.

If you've read <u>The Four Agreements</u>, <u>The Celestine Prophecy</u>, and a multitude of other great books devoted to self-improvement, self-empowerment and success, and yet you still find yourself facing limitations and lack in any areas of your life, this book is for you.

Let me be clear: Our personal libraries are filled with deeply profound books that offer eternal truths and wisdom we can trust and rely upon. They all offer time-tested techniques for success, self-fulfillment, joy, love and inner peace.

Just as all roads lead to Rome, all of these books can get us to the same place of success and self-satisfaction if we use the tools effectively and we apply the concepts consistently.

Unfortunately, many of us don't do this. We buy a book, but only read parts of it. Or we read it from cover to cover, but don't apply the principles in our daily lives.

Or we apply the principles, but give up before we've established them as habits and routines, such that we don't manifest the results promised by the authors.

Or we have incorporated the principles into our daily habits and routines, but still haven't gotten the results we desire.

Regardless of the scenario involved, when we finally acknowledge that our efforts have failed us and that our latest self-help book is not the Holy Grail of answers to our prayers, we put aside the book and move onto the next book, the next philosophy, the next technique, the next guru, with new hope that our next effort will finally, magically, deliver to us what we're seeking.

Unfortunately, the expression "Insanity is doing the same thing and expecting different results" is extremely relevant here: If there is something blocking us, something getting in the way of our success and self-fulfillment, independent of the books and techniques that we're using, then it doesn't matter how many books or CDs we buy, or how many seminars and conferences we attend, we are going to continue to fail until we correct the underlying problem.

This book, <u>Forgive To Win!</u>, will do just that. <u>Forgive To Win!</u> will finally put an end to your uphill struggle for health, wealth, happiness, or whatever it is that you seek.

THE MISSING LINK

So what is the missing link? Why is it that we are motivated to change, and we work hard at it, and yet we do not succeed at attaining our goals?

It's because we sabotage ourselves. We sabotage our best efforts. We procrastinate.

We resist. We don't follow direction. We don't follow through. We allow ourselves to be distracted and derailed.

We sabotage ourselves in a variety of ways, such that we perpetually withhold from ourselves all the goodies the universe has to offer, blaming it all the while on bad luck or it being someone else's fault, rather than acknowledging that we are the Prime Movers of our destiny, that we are responsible for the lack and limitations in our lives, and nobody else.

On a conscious level we want to win, but on a deep, unconscious level, we are filled with guilt, shame, self-condemnation, and self-loathing, such that, rather than believing that we are worthy of winning and deserving of abundance and success, we believe that we are sinners deserving of punishment, suffering and failure. All of this is below our conscious awareness.

Our subconscious mind, intent on manifesting what we believe about ourselves at a deeply-embedded, unconscious level, believes our own harsh judgments about ourselves, and punishes us for our "sins." It does this by sabotaging our conscious efforts.

It generates resistance and roadblocks. It attracts inferior elements. It encourages miscommunication, chaos, and confusion. The end result is an external world that reflects our internal self-concept. The end result is our not getting what we want.

The only way to reverse this process, in order to generate success and prosperity, is to put an end to our guilt, shame and self-loathing by forgiving and loving ourselves. The only way to do this is to first forgive and love others. This is what <u>Forgive To Win!</u>'s Forgiveness Diet has been designed to accomplish.

THE FORGIVENESS DIET

The Forgiveness Diet is a structured program that trains our mind to engage in behaviors that will benefit us in the long run. More specifically, the Forgiveness Diet is a daily regimen of thoughts, actions and exercises devoted to extending unconditional forgiveness, acceptance, and love. It is a daily regimen of estimable acts of kindness and service to others.

When we have mastered the Forgiveness Diet, our subconscious mind will believe we are good enough and worthy of reward, at which point it will stop sabotaging our efforts and start constructing the synchronistic attraction of synergistic people and circumstances that will favor our prosperity and success in all realms.

> *The Forgiveness Diet is the ultimate prosperity principle!*

The reason why many of us have difficulty believing this is true is because we've been trained to believe that nice guys finish last, that no good deed goes unpunished, and that love, kindness and forgiveness are for chumps and suckers.

Nothing could be further from the truth. These are self-destructive messages generated by our subconscious mind to support its self-sabotaging agenda to derail us from healing ourselves and attracting abundance into our lives.

Although it is obvious that many people who are loathsome, selfish, unloving and hurtful towards others have succeeded and prospered, for most of us who mean no harm to others, emulating people like that will not deliver us what we want.

If we repair ourselves by extending unconditional forgiveness, acceptance and love to everyone, under all circumstances, without exceptions, we can replace our self-loathing with self-loving, thereby putting an end to our self-sabotage, such that our subconscious mind works with us rather than against us to attract and manifest everything we've ever wanted.

The best part about the Forgiveness Diet is that we don't need to understand it for it to work. We don't even need to believe it. Additionally, we don't need to gain any deep insights about ourselves in order to get results.

We just need to do it. We just need to implement a few basic behaviors and practices on a consistent basis until they become habits.

But don't take my word for it. Take the Forgive To Win! 90-Day Challenge. Rather than rejecting the Forgiveness Diet as magical or wishful thinking without giving it a try, follow it rigorously for 90 days and find out for yourself what it has to offer.

Make the decision to put aside your skepticism, negativity, cynicism and doubt for 90 days in order to work the program as vigorously and as honestly as you possibly can.

What have you got to lose? What's 90 days in the bigger scheme of things? What's 90 days in the expanse and duration of your life? It's nothing. So what if you spend 90 days being generous, esteeming others, and forgiving them their trespasses? What's the downside? There really isn't any.

If you decide after 90 days that the experience was not transformative and was a complete waste of time, which I guarantee won't be the case, you will have the rest of your life to be angry, vengeful, withholding, thoughtless, selfish and self-centered, and to see where that gets you.

But if I'm right in encouraging you to devote a mere 90 days of your life to the Forgiveness Diet, you will greatly appreciate the experience you put yourself through, you will see fewer roadblocks and potholes appearing in your life, you will be happier, more productive, and more successful, and you will gladly continue to engage in the Forgiveness Diet program.

That being said, there are two additional points to appreciate:

(1) The components of the Forgiveness Diet do not, for the most part, embrace any radically-new concepts or present any groundbreaking techniques.

What makes the Forgiveness Diet unique and invaluable is the organization of the concepts and techniques into a structured, disciplined daily program designed to serve one purpose: to train ourselves to love ourselves by loving and forgiving others.

In the process of doing this, we eliminate our self-loathing, self-sabotaging behaviors which have been getting in the way of our success.

(2) For those of us wondering if we will sabotage our efforts at implementing the Forgiveness Diet, just as we have sabotaged our efforts with other self-help books, the answer is that many of us will try.

Here's the distinction: With other self-help books, when we attempt to re-visit them, after having put them aside, essentially nothing has changed. We approach each new effort with the same self-sabotaging subconscious mind generating the same self-sabotaging resistance, the result being one more failed attempt.

However, with Forgive To Win!, every time we re-visit the material after having resisted it, we actually decrease our self-loathing and increase our self-esteem, to some degree, because that's what happens when we focus our attention on compassion, acceptance, and forgiveness.

This results in a reduction of resistance, such that, with every new effort, it is more likely that we will succeed at getting through the material and integrating the concepts into our daily routines.

CHAPTER 1

WHAT IT IS: AN OVERVIEW

Our subconscious mind manifests reality from our thoughts, based upon what it believes we believe about ourselves at a very deep, unconscious level.

If we have thoughts of shame, guilt, self-condemnation and self-loathing deeply embedded in our unconscious mind, these thoughts will generate self-sabotage and interfere with our efforts to create a prosperous and satisfying life for ourselves.

SELF-SABOTAGE

We sabotage ourselves in a variety of ways. We avoid doing things that are in our best interests. We procrastinate and don't follow through. We engage in behaviors that are harmful at worst and non-productive at best.

Each of us has our own personal list of counter-productive, self-destructive, self-sabotaging behaviors that have been getting in our way for years, generating poor health, poor relationships, unfulfilling jobs, financial limitations, and a longing for love, happiness and contentment which forever seem beyond our reach.

We will discuss in Chapter 2 how our thoughts create our reality, the varieties and subtleties of our self-sabotage, and the root causes of our deeply-embedded self-loathing which generate the self-sabotaging behaviors.

SELF-SOLUTION

If our deeply-embedded self-loathing is the problem, then learning to esteem ourselves and love ourselves is the solution.

In order to esteem ourselves, we need to esteem others. We do this by engaging in estimable acts of kindness and by being of service to others without needing or wanting anything in return.

ESTIMABLE ACTS

When we engage in estimable acts of kindness and are of service to others, offering our support and assistance when they are in need, and providing resources to help them navigate the difficulties in their lives, it increases our self-esteem.

Conversely, when we stop being selfish, withholding, oppositional and obstructive in our transactions with others, it increases our self-esteem.

Additionally, when we let go of anger, resentments, judgments, and jealousies, extending unconditional forgiveness, acceptance and love instead, that, too, increases our self-esteem.

As our self-esteem increases by repeatedly and consistently engaging in these behaviors without needing anything in return, it alters the balance between that part of our mind that believes we are worthy (deserving of success and rewards) and that part of our mind that believes we are worthless (deserving of failure and punishment).

Over time, our subconscious mind starts believing that we are good enough and deserving of success, prosperity, and happiness, to the point of decreasing its efforts to sabotage us and increasing its efforts to generate positive outcomes in our lives.

Unfortunately, due to the massive amount of deeply-embedded guilt and shame which keeps the fires of self-loathing roaring deeply within, engaging in estimable acts of kindness is not sufficient, by itself, to truly end our self-sabotage.

For our subconscious mind to fully believe that we are deserving of reward, not punishment, such that it starts working with our conscious mind rather than against it, it must believe we have not just esteemed ourselves by right-minded thoughts and actions, but that we have forgiven ourselves as well for our perceived past transgressions buried deeply in our psyche.

Truth be told, regardless of the quantity and quality of estimable acts we offer others, unless we find a way to forgive ourselves, we will never put an end to the guilt, shame and self-loathing, and the self-sabotage that goes with them.

So now the question becomes: How do we forgive ourselves?

THE POWER OF FORGIVENESS

It is impossible for us to forgive ourselves directly because of the magnitude of our unconscious guilt and shame which cannot be overridden by our conscious will.

Fortunately, there is a mechanism that enables us to forgive ourselves by forgiving others, which is something each of us is capable of doing.

That mechanism is called projection. It is an unconscious process that is designed by our ego mind to reduce unconscious guilt, anxiety and conflict generated by our own faults, flaws and imperfections.

Here's how it works: Regardless of how badly people have behaved in the past or are presently behaving, when we judge them harshly and perceive them in a negative light, we are actually projecting onto them our own unconscious, harsh, negative judgments of ourselves.

By perceiving them, rather than ourselves, as guilty, flawed and unworthy, it essentially takes our unconscious mind off of any bad feelings about ourselves that would otherwise leak into our conscious awareness and generate anxiety. Unfortunately, although we may be less anxious and feel less guilty as a result of our projections, this doesn't reduce the guilt and shame which generate our deeply-embedded self-loathing. It just hides it from our conscious awareness.

That being said, here's how we use projection to our advantage: When we stop judging others and choose to perceive them in a forgiving and loving light instead, we are actually forgiving our projections onto them of our own guilt and self-loathing, which is another way of saying we are forgiving ourselves.

As we forgive ourselves, our self-esteem increases and our self-sabotage decreases. Consequently, if we forgive others consistently and repeatedly, the reality we manifest in our lives will be one of success and abundance, reflecting our self-love rather than our self-disdain.

We will explore in Chapter 3 a variety of estimable acts of kindness that are available to us, and we will discuss this process of forgiving our projections in order to forgive ourselves, esteem ourselves and end our self-sabotage.

THE PROCESS OF FORGIVENESS

We will discuss in Chapter 4 the process of forgiving others, as well as the difficulties we will encounter because of our unwillingness to let go of our judgments despite knowing that it's in our best interests to do so.

We will explore a variety of forgiveness techniques and perspectives, including ways to look at the offending situations and offenders differently, in order to transcend our ego, let go of our judgments, and overcome our resistance to forgive.

We will discuss the concept of "Forgive and forget."

We will address forgiving others who have injured us in the past, forgiving others who injure us in the present, and forgiving others our judgments of them, whether they have actually done something to us or not.

This latter scenario is the most complex of all and the most important, because the first two usually involve a limited number of people, whereas the third involves a great many people we deal with everyday who we project our guilt and self-loathing onto with our judgments.

We will discuss the power of gratitude in the forgiveness process and the value of recognizing blessings in disguise.

We will discuss how hanging onto anger hurts us physically and emotionally, and how forgiveness heals us in those realms as well.

THE FORGIVENESS DIET

We will present in Chapter 5 an organized, self-empowerment program called the Forgiveness Diet, a daily regimen of thoughts, actions, and exercises designed to establish new thought-emotion-behavior habits of esteeming, accepting, forgiving and being of service to others.

This daily regimen includes, in addition to engaging in estimable acts, letting go of judgments, resentments and anger, and forgiving others their trespasses, past and present: (1) Morning Mindfulness Calisthenics & Mindfulness Reminders, (2) Forgiveness Mantras to repeat throughout the day, (3) an evening Forgiveness Inventory to evaluate how we did each day in terms of our estimable acts and the forgiving of others, (4) a Forgiveness Inventory List that addresses what and who we need to focus on during the following day, (5) a Gratitude List, (6) Forgiveness Affirmations, (7) Forgiveness Visualizations, (8) Synchronistic Contemplations, which relate to the Collective Unconscious, where all minds are joined and the Law of Attraction is set into motion, (9) Dream Programming and Lucid Dreaming, and (10) Rating Scales to monitor our success with the Forgiveness Diet.

We will discuss the importance of engaging in the Forgiveness Diet for a minimum of 90 days, which is a sufficient amount of time to make it an established habit in our lives and to start seeing the positive results we desire.

We will also discuss the importance of not getting impatient, frustrated, angry, anxious, depressed or discouraged if our lives don't improve as fast as we would like them to. The positive transformation of our lives, as we eliminate our self-sabotaging behaviors, will involve a variety of people and circumstances coming together, the synchronization of which is not something in our control.

What is in our control is our commitment, persistence, and perseverance. If we are patient and stick with the Forgiveness Diet, we will, in time, discover rewards far greater than we ever could have imagined.

GETTING EVERYTHING YOU WANT!

Once the Forgiveness Diet has been firmly established as a daily habit, such that engaging in estimable acts, letting go of judgments, and forgiving others are as automatic as washing our hands or brushing our teeth, we then have the option of implementing a Success Diet, which can be easily integrated into the routines of the Forgiveness Diet with little additional time demands, in order to accelerate the accomplishment of our goals.

We will discuss in Chapter 6 the Success Diet plan.

CHAPTER 2

SELF-LOATHING & SELF-SABOTAGE

We are not victims of a hostile or chaotic universe. It is our thoughts that create our experiences. It is our subconscious mind that is the engineer in this regard, driving our destiny towards success or failure.

If we believe, at a core level of our identity, deeply-embedded in our unconscious mind, that we are "good enough" and worthy of success, then our subconscious mind will believe this as well, and it will use all its powers to manifest the success, prosperity, health and happiness we desire by synergizing with our conscious mind, such that wise rather than reckless decisions are made, opportunities are taken advantage of, rather than avoided or squandered, and all forms of self-sabotage which might be possible are simply not entertained.

However, if we believe at a core level of our identity, deeply-embedded in our unconscious mind, that we are not good enough and that we are not worthy of success, our subconscious mind will believe this as well and devote all its powers to sabotaging us and keeping us imprisoned in a physical and emotional world full of suffering, scarcity, lack and limitation.

When our subconscious mind is working against our conscious efforts to succeed and be happy, because of the guilt, shame, self-condemnation and self-loathing buried deep in our psyche, it whispers in our ear thoughts of failure and futility, as well as a variety of negative messages and labels designed to derail our motivation, our drive, and our commitment to success.

Some of the messages we receive from our subconscious inner critic include:

"There's no point in trying." "It will never work." "Something will go wrong." "You're better off doing something else." "It's a waste of time, so why bother?"

Taking these messages to heart, we get demoralized and depressed. We yield to the negativity. We generate a variety of self-sabotaging behaviors that alienate people, block our efforts, and keep us from the life we want.

> "The fault, dear Brutus, lies not in our stars, but in ourselves that we are underlings."
> -William Shakespeare

It is important that we identify our self-sabotaging behaviors and appreciate the different things we do consciously and unconsciously that interfere with our success. They are all within our control. We have the power to not do them.

Here's a list of some of the more common self-sabotaging behaviors:

- We sabotage ourselves when we don't do things that we know are in our best interests, when we make excuses, when we create dramas that distract us, and when we procrastinate.
- We sabotage ourselves when we fail to complete projects or when we leave them to the last minute, and then rush to complete them, thereby not putting forth our best efforts.
- We sabotage ourselves when we aren't prepared.
- We sabotage ourselves when we isolate ourselves from our friends and loved ones.

- We sabotage ourselves when we avoid meeting new people and cultivating new relationships.
- We sabotage ourselves when we desire to meet a significant other, but do nothing to encourage the process.
- We sabotage ourselves when we turn down invitations.
- We sabotage ourselves when we accept invitations and show up at the events, but then behave in ways that give people a bad impression of us and generate in them an unwillingness to get to know us better.

We are masters of our fate or victims of our folly.

- We sabotage ourselves when we're late for appointments. For most of us, being late is usually not due to traffic or some other unanticipated circumstance. It's usually a function of choices we make, such as not allowing enough time to get done what needs to be done before leaving, not being disciplined enough to leave when we know it's time to go, or not adequately factoring in time for unexpected contingencies that invariably present themselves, traffic being just one of them.

Oftentimes, we don't mind allowing ourselves to be late because we believe if we offer up an "acceptable" excuse, such as getting stuck in traffic, we'll be let off the hook and there will be no significant consequences.

Unfortunately, this is faulty logic. We're just fooling ourselves by feeding ourselves such rationalizations, which is part of the self-sabotaging process.

In truth, when we allow ourselves to be late, we are essentially saying to the person or people waiting for us that we don't care that much about respecting them or their time. This can have negative consequences, in terms of disinclining them to cooperate with us.

Equally so, when we allow ourselves to be late, we're also essentially saying that we don't care that much about respecting ourselves, being reliable and accountable, and maintaining the integrity of our reputation.

Being late is breaking a promise. It's not fulfilling a contract to convene at a specific time. It refutes the concept that our word is our bond. Insofar as being punctual is an act of consideration, when we aren't punctual, it can stop the flow of positive energy and discourage people from supporting us and going the distance.

Although it is likely that when we are occasionally late it is not held against us, it is, nonetheless, an off-putting event. When there is a pattern of being late, it is highly likely to have a negative impact, to some degree, on our personal and business relationships.

- We sabotage ourselves when we don't return phone calls or we don't call people back in a timely fashion. It's inconsiderate behavior. It's a breach of an understood social contract. It puts people off. It sets the stage for a future event when they might be in a position to help us, but won't because of our previous bad behaviors.

- We sabotage ourselves when we agree to do something and then don't do it, such as making a commitment to appear at an event and then not showing up.

By our present actions or inactions, we weave our future's tapestry.

- We sabotage ourselves when we let things fall into disrepair and don't engage in preventive maintenance.
- We sabotage ourselves when we're disorganized.
- We sabotage ourselves when we forget to write things down that we need to do, and then we forget to do them.
- We sabotage ourselves when we play it safe and we don't take reasonable risks.
- We sabotage ourselves when we blame others and don't take responsibility for our actions.
- We sabotage ourselves when we buy things we can't afford and/or don't really need.
- We sabotage ourselves when we find ourselves in unhealthy places or circumstances, and then we participate rather than disengage.
- We sabotage ourselves when we overindulge in activities and substances that have immediate gratification but provide no long-term sustenance.

Some examples of this include spending excessive amounts of time on the computer, watching TV, or playing video games instead of improving ourselves and pursuing our goals.

Other examples include excessively eating, drinking, and drugging ourselves. These behaviors are sabotaging not simply because they are empty calories, so to speak, but because they are self-destructive choices that damage us physically, emotionally, cognitively, and spiritually, to the degree of seriously impairing our ability to focus, to initiate, to self-motivate and to succeed.

Whenever we overwhelm our senses with substances that alter our minds and bodies, it may be entertaining and have some value, but over the long run such behavior is abusive because it damages our brain, depresses our immune system, contributes to accidents and injuries, derails our motivation and drive, and usually consumes a lot of time, energy and money that could be better spent elsewhere.

This isn't about not indulging in any behaviors that are fun or mindless. It's simply about making sure we're not damaging ourselves or our goals in the process.

- We sabotage ourselves when we make poor food choices, which include animal products, non-organic products, processed foods, junk foods, foods which contain artificial substances and chemical preservatives, and foods which contain excessive amounts of salt, sugar and fat. We sabotage ourselves when we ignore the value of vitamins and nutritional supplements.
- We sabotage ourselves when we don't get enough exercise.
- We sabotage ourselves when we don't get enough sleep or we sleep too much.
- We sabotage ourselves when we get caught up in our ego, which is always keeping score, always wanting more, and always thinking, "What's in it for me?"

This behavior of focusing solely on our own needs, without having any empathy regarding the needs of others and the trials and tribulations they may be experiencing, is sabotaging because it deprives us of our connection to humanity, it contributes to our core sense of guilt and shame, and it keeps us in a contracted state that shuts off the flow of positive energy and love.

Ebenezer Scrooge, in Charles Dickens' A Christmas Carol, focused on himself, amassed a great fortune, but led an empty, bitter life until he opened up his heart and mind, and then chose to share his success with those less fortunate.

> We are the ultimate architects of our destiny.

- We sabotage ourselves when we spend time with people who are mindless, abusive or toxic.

- We sabotage ourselves when we spend time with people who influence us to maintain the status quo or go down unhealthy or non-productive paths, rather than spending time with people who challenge us, encourage us, nurture us, support us, and inspire us to move in the direction of greater happiness, success and well-being.

   When we choose to not seek out healthy, proactive role models who can enlighten and guide us, and instead choose to hang out with people who are negative, pessimistic, angry, judgmental, close-minded, uninspiring, lacking in ambition, lacking in virtue, or paralyzed and immobilized by their own poor choices and their belief in their victimhood, we are making a monumental mistake which will undoubtedly have a negative impact on our lives.

   It is critical that we appreciate that no matter how entertaining it might be, it is massive self-sabotage when we cooperate with inferior elements. The people we spend time with define us and either contribute to our growth and progress or contribute to our stagnation and decline.

- We sabotage ourselves when, fueled by our desire for pleasure and immediate gratification, we make short-sighted and impulsive decisions without considering all the consequences of our actions.

- We sabotage ourselves when we dwell on the past or the future at the expense of living in the Now. When we are preoccupied with what was or what will be, we are in a state of contracted awareness which dampens our creative and intuitive processes, and which leads to missed opportunities and insights.

ACCIDENTS HAPPEN?

- We sabotage ourselves when we're driving on the freeway, caught up in our thoughts, talking on our cell phone, or text messaging, and not fully attending to other drivers and conditions on the road, insofar as these behaviors can lead to accidents.

Truth be told, if we crash our car because we were distracted by something we were doing, it is a misnomer to call it an accident. It's something that could have been avoided if we had exercised better judgment.

- We sabotage ourselves when we're tailgating. It doesn't even require that we not be paying attention. If something unexpected happens while we're tailgating, and the car in front of us stops abruptly, the laws of physics kick in, we are unable to brake in time no matter how quickly we might respond, and the result is a rear-end collision.

  Although we will refer to it as an accident, it's not. It's another example of our creating a negative reality for ourselves because of our poor judgment.

- Many "accidents" happen in the workplace. But, again, if we look closely, they aren't really accidents. They could have been avoided.

  For example: Perhaps we're angry at our boss, frustrated with our job, overworked and underpaid, worried about getting fired or laid off, and/or worried about making the next mortgage payment.

  Or perhaps we're thinking about a relationship that is going south, a fight we had with a loved one, or resentments and grievances we're harboring towards others.

  Caught up in our anxiety, anger, depression, or fear, we are inattentive and distracted, such that we don't see the spilled coffee on the floor, for example, and we slip, fall to the ground and injure ourselves in the process.

  We can call it an accident if we want, but it would be more accurate to acknowledge that, had we been paying closer attention, the "accident" and its consequences most likely never would have happened.

  These are but a few examples. There are many things that happen in our lives which we refer to as accidents or bad luck, which, in truth, are the result of poor judgment, sloppy behavior, and not being fully present, focused and vigilant.

DON'T SHOOT THE MESSENGER.

- We sabotage ourselves when someone tells us something we don't want to hear, and, instead of taking it to heart, we attempt to invalidate their message by attacking them. This is a mistake.

  Shooting the messenger prevents us from dealing with a truth that could help us make better choices and improve our lives.

- We sabotage ourselves when we engage in "contempt prior to investigation," which means we prejudge and reject an idea without first evaluating it to determine if it might have validity.

> *We sabotage ourselves when we don't choose love and truth to guide our lives.*

- We sabotage ourselves when we react to loved ones with anger, verbal abuse and other forms of aggression or passive-aggression, all of which tend to push away from us the very people with whom we want to establish and/or maintain close, nurturing relationships.

- We sabotage ourselves when we choose to stay hurt, resentful, angry and unforgiving over past transgressions of others, because, in the long run, anger is bad for our physical, emotional, and spiritual health.

  Suffice it to say that hanging onto any negative emotions after the inciting incident has passed is self-sabotage because negative emotions of any kind: (1) are hazardous to our well-being in general, (2) can distract us and lead to accidents and injuries, (3) can cause us to impulsively say and do things that aren't in our best interests, and (4) can discourage others from interacting and cooperating with us.

- We sabotage ourselves when we judge and criticize others, whether it be in thought, in words, in body language or other actions, subtle or otherwise, and regardless of how they have behaved or are behaving, because indulging in any form of negativity towards others is an attack, and any attack, even when justified in some way in our mind, contributes to our guilt, shame, self-condemnation, and self-loathing, which further reinforces our subconscious belief that we are unworthy and do not deserve abundance and rewards.

- We sabotage ourselves when we see a list of self-sabotaging behaviors, recognize that we are guilty of engaging in many of them, acknowledge that they are getting in the way of our success and happiness, and yet do not make a commitment to put an end to them.

The key to ending all of our self-sabotaging behaviors is to end our self-loathing, which is their underlying cause.

SELF-LOATHING

Although most of us aren't aware that we are self-loathing, and would deny it if accused of it by others, the bottom line is this: If we aren't getting the life we want, we're sabotaging ourselves. And if we're sabotaging ourselves, it's because, despite appearances, despite the fact that we may value and admire ourselves in any number of ways, we are self-loathing.

Our self-loathing stems from extremely harsh, shaming, condemning and guilt-generating labels about ourselves that are deeply-embedded in our unconscious mind, which whisper incessantly to us (at an unconscious level) that we are unworthy, undeserving, unlovable, bad, stupid, thoughtless, unkind, unloving, selfish, greedy, sinful, and guilty, deserving of punishment (not reward), hell, (not heaven), and eternal pain and suffering (not relief and deliverance).

Where do the guilt, shame, and self-condemnations come from? There are several possibilities. Maybe they are the result of shame, guilt, and low self-esteem messages (verbal and non-verbal) communicated to us by our parents, other caregivers, our instructors, our siblings, and our peers, intentionally or otherwise, when we were very young.

Unfortunately, our parents, in particular, are the prime movers of much of our shame, guilt and self-condemnations, not because our parents were evil and hurtful people, but because they didn't know any better.

Most parents simply don't know how to be effective parents and not scar their children.

Most parents have poor communication skills and are not in touch with their emotions and unconscious motivations, such that they unintentionally end up repeating the same dysfunctional behaviors that they were exposed to as children.

Here's an example: When a small child shows a parent a drawing he's done, and the parent dismisses the child, too busy working or watching TV to take the time to look at the drawing, it is shameful and demeaning to the child, and it sends the child the message that he or she isn't really all that special or important to the parent, despite this not being the case and despite all the nurturing things the parent has done for the child in the past.

When the parent does something thoughtless and shaming like this, and doesn't repair it with an apology and appropriate attention, the child's self-esteem is damaged. This is called an empathic break occurring during the child's identity formation.

As these empathic breaks repeat themselves over time and aren't repaired, the child eventually puts two and two together and comes up with six: "I must not be good enough. I must be stupid. I must be a nuisance. I must have done something bad or wrong. I must not be loveable. I must deserve them ignoring me and treating me so badly."

It all happens at an unconscious, non-verbal level. The child's mind doesn't have the capacity to adequately evaluate the situation. The child can't appreciate that perhaps the parent's behavior has nothing to do with them, that perhaps the parent is distracted and unreceptive due to being tired, anxious, or frustrated, and is taking it out on him (or her) inappropriately.

Instead, the child assumes the worst about himself. The child assumes that the parent isn't the one with the problem, but rather that he is.

Over time, the shame, guilt and negative self-perceptions build and grow until the child's dysfunctional personality and low self-esteem have been firmly established, regardless of how accomplished and confident the child might appear to be.

Eventually, the child becomes an adult with guilt, shame, and self-loathing neuroses at the core of his identity, and with a subconscious mind dedicated to sabotage and self-destruction in one or more areas of his life.

That being said, perhaps our guilt, shame, and self-loathing have nothing to do with early childhood development. Perhaps they have to do with poor choices we've made in the past as adolescents or adults, which have been hurtful, abusive and unloving towards others, and have left us with bad feelings about ourselves and a core belief that we deserve to be punished rather than rewarded.

Perhaps the guilt, shame and self-loathing have to do with poor choices we've made in past lives, our karma catching up to us, leaving us with core feelings of unworthiness and self-recriminations that we're not even remotely aware of.

Perhaps the guilt, shame and self-loathing have to do with genetic memories locked in our DNA and RNA from our ancestors that got neuro-chemically integrated into our personality and our sense of self.

Perhaps our guilt, shame and self-loathing have to do with the unconscious belief that we have sinned against God and that He will punish us with eternal damnation.

Perhaps it's all of the above. Perhaps it's none of the above.

Fortunately, it doesn't matter why we loathe ourselves or how it started. What matters is that we stop it because it is generating self-sabotaging behaviors that are keeping us from the life we want.

Fortunately, we don't need insight into the origins of our self-loathing in order to put an end to it. All we need to do is reprogram our unconscious mind to love ourselves rather than loathe ourselves, at which point our subconscious mind will end its self-sabotaging behaviors and work towards fulfilling our deepest desires.

So that becomes the task at hand: to put an end to our self-loathing by learning how to love ourselves.

CHAPTER 3

ESTIMABLE ACTS & FORGIVENESS

If self-condemnation and self-loathing at a deep, unconscious level are the cause of our self-sabotage and the lack and limitations in our lives which goes with them, then the only way to end our self-sabotage and succeed, once and for all, is for us to esteem ourselves and love ourselves instead.

This is not a simple task. We must earn our own love by convincing our subconscious mind that we are loving human beings. We do this by esteeming and loving others. We demonstrate our esteem and love for others by being of service to others, by engaging in estimable acts of kindness.

We demonstrate to our subconscious mind that we are caring and compassionate people, that we are generous with our time, our energy and our resources, that we assist those in need as best we can, and that we put our own needs aside, expecting nothing in return.

Over time, as we repeatedly, consistently and persistently do this, our self-esteem increases.

THE END OF SELF-SABOTAGE

As our self-esteem increases, our guilt, shame and self-condemnations recede into the background. Our subconscious mind starts getting the message that we like ourselves, that we're proud of ourselves, and that we believe we deserve prosperity and success in all aspects of our lives.

Eventually, our subconscious mind starts believing in our goodness and worthiness as well, and, rather than sabotaging and defeating us like it has done in the past, it starts cooperating with our conscious mind to help us attract and manifest the reality we want with all the success and prosperity that we desire.

Instead of facilitating procrastination, resistance, oppositional behaviors, reckless, impulsive behaviors and other forms of disabling negativity, sabotage and failure, it orchestrates proactivity, efficiency, effectiveness, cooperation, synergy, synchronicity, and success.

So that becomes the task at hand: On a daily basis, we engage in estimable acts of kindness towards others. We constantly look for opportunities to be of service to others, to improve the quality of their lives, and to bring light and love into their world, whether they be family, friends, employers, co-workers, peers, acquaintances, or strangers.

Patience. Persistence. Perseverance.

If we are to succeed beyond our wildest dreams by utilizing the principles endorsed in this book, then we must make estimable acts of kindness a huge priority in our lives.

Not just whenever it's convenient. Not just when other people are watching. It's got to be 24-7, to the point where estimable acts of kindness are what we do and who we are, end of story.

A word to the wise: This is no quick scheme. It will take time to undo old patterns. Consequently, we must remain diligent, committed, and self-motivated. If we do this and if we patiently persist and persevere, we will succeed.

ESTIMABLE ACTS

When people ask for help, we graciously consent and cooperate as best we can.

When people don't ask for help, we don't wait for an invitation. If we see they are in need, we step up to the plate and offer our assistance.

As for those who cross our path who seem to not need our help, we still engage in estimable acts: We greet them warmly, we make eye contact, we exchange pleasantries, and, if something occurs to us that might be of benefit, we mention it.

And so we offer assistance to whomever we encounter, no matter what the situation or the circumstances. We make no judgments. We provide assistance without requiring explanations, without any conditions or exceptions, and with no expectations.

We help others, even if it's inconvenient for us, even if it takes up time and energy that we would have preferred expending elsewhere, and even if we perceive we could have put our time and energy to better use.

Bottom line: There is no better use of our time and energy than to esteem and be of service to others.

Why? Because, in the long run, by our selfless efforts, we will eliminate our self-loathing and pave the way for our subconscious mind to manifest our dreams and deliver to us the life that we want.

Try it, you'll like it!

There are an endless number of tasks, favors, and behaviors we engage in that qualify as estimable acts of kindness. Holding the door for someone is an estimable act. Holding the elevator for someone is an estimable act.

Giving someone a lift who doesn't have transportation is an estimable act. Helping someone fix a flat tire is an estimable act.

Helping someone carry packages to their car is an estimable act. Helping someone move into a new apartment or house is an estimable act.

Being patient and pleasant while waiting on line is an estimable act. Letting someone go ahead of you in line is an estimable act. Letting someone change lanes on the freeway is an estimable act.

Picking trash off the ground that you didn't put there is an estimable act.

Anticipating that someone needs something and then getting it for them is an estimable act.

Giving or loaning money or possessions is an estimable act.

Essentially, any act of kindness towards others that comes from the heart is an estimable act.

Any act that respects other people, regardless of differences or circumstances, is an estimable act.

Following the Golden Rule of treating people as we wish to be treated is an estimable act. Turning the other cheek is an estimable act.

Acknowledging when we are wrong, apologizing and making amends is an estimable act.

Not keeping score as to who has done what to whom and who owes what to whom is an estimable act.

Finding something positive to say about everyone we meet is an estimable act.

Offering a helpful suggestion to someone is an estimable act.

Encouraging and inspiring people to stay positive is an estimable act.

Not spreading gossip is an estimable act.

Telling the truth is an estimable act.

Keeping commitments is an estimable act. Not being late is an estimable act.

Not sweating the small stuff is an estimable act.

Giving the benefit of the doubt is an estimable act.

Being tolerant and overlooking people's flaws and imperfections is an estimable act.

Overlooking minor transgressions is an estimable act.

Not assuming the worst and giving people the benefit of the doubt is an estimable act.

Listening when others speak, without interrupting, is an estimable act.

Respecting other people's boundaries is an estimable act.

Validating other people's feelings, even if we don't agree with them, is an estimable act.

Being empathetic is an estimable act.

Advocating for others who can't advocate for themselves is an estimable act.

Respecting animals, plants and inanimate objects, as much as is practical and reasonable to do, is an estimable act.

Giving someone you care for a hug or a kiss for no particular reason except to acknowledge your affection and support is an estimable act.

Giving someone you care for a hug or a kiss in the middle of an argument to derail the negative energy and remind each other of the love that exists despite the quarreling and negative feelings is an estimable act.

Letting go of our judgments, our biases, and our assumptions about others, and choosing instead to accept them as they are, without needing to change them, is an estimable act.

Extending unconditional forgiveness is an estimable act.

THERE CAN BE NO EXCEPTIONS!

We withhold our kindness and consideration from no one. We treat everyone equally, appreciating that everyone deserves our compassion and our grace.

If we don't do this, if we judge some people as undeserving of our compassion, and we withhold our acts of kindness from them, we are punishing ourselves more than them. This is true because, by withholding estimable acts of kindness from anyone, we are essentially attacking them with our judgments and our withholding, in which case, rather than building our self-esteem, we are eroding it, increasing our self-loathing, and reinforcing the messages that lead to self-sabotage.

The point is this: No matter how many estimable acts we have engaged in, if we withhold our kindnesses from specific people, even just one person, our subconscious mind will hang onto that one exception as proof that we are unloving and undeserving, and will use it to crucify us with self-sabotage and failure.

If we truly want to succeed at this, there can be no exceptions. Regardless of the circumstance, we withhold our compassion and service from no one, including those who we don't like, as well as those who have treated us poorly in the past.

This is a critical point. We can't pick and choose who we'll be kind to if we want to eliminate our self-loathing. We must not allow past hurts and resentments to get in the way of our efforts to serve others with love and generosity.

THERE CAN BE NO CONDITIONS!

Our estimable acts of kindness to others must always be done unconditionally, without expecting anything in return. If we put conditions on the kindness and generosity we show to others, it's still kindness and generosity that obviously is meritorious, but it's no longer an estimable act in the therapeutic context we're discussing here.

When we are motivated to do something out of self-interest instead of out of the goodness of our heart, it can no longer be considered a pure act of service to others. It is now an act of our ego, serving our ego's agenda. This will not increase our self-esteem.

Our subconscious mind will take any condition or expectation of reciprocity on our part that we impose on our giving as proof that we are not truly loving and not truly worthy.

Here's how it works: Any condition or expectation as to how someone should respond to our kindness is a judgment. Judgments are attacks on others. Attacks on others make us feel bad about ourselves and further reinforce our guilt, shame, self-condemnation and self-loathing.

Consequently, it's best we don't expect an acknowledgement or a thank you for what we do. If we should happen to get a thank you, that's nice. But if we don't get one, we don't cop an attitude, we don't generate a resentment, we don't get all holier-than-thou, because if we do, then our giving was conditional and ego-based, and will contribute to our embedded belief that we are manipulative, self-serving, and disingenuous, thereby increasing our guilt, shame and self-loathing rather than decreasing them.

Equally true: If we offer to help another, but make them feel that it is a burden, that we are doing them a big favor and that we'd really rather be doing something else than helping them, we are sabotaging our game plan and defeating ourselves.

By indicating that we are being inconvenienced in some way, we are not being gracious and considerate. We have allowed our ego to enter the equation. When that happens, any increase in our self-esteem that might have resulted from our estimable act is neutralized by the loss of self-esteem generated by our ungracious, unloving behavior.

So it really is critical that if we decide to do something nice for someone else, we do it willingly, wholeheartedly, and without any reluctance or lack of grace.

Additionally, if we do something kind and thoughtful for someone, such as graciously taking out the garbage when it's not our turn, for example, but while we're doing it, we're thinking hostile, resentful thoughts about that person, we're neutralizing any positive effect on our self-esteem because of our judgmental attack thoughts, even if they're not aware of them.

THE POWER OF FORGIVENESS

Although estimable acts are necessary, in order to replace the negative messages and labels about ourselves with positive messages of self-admiration and self-esteem, they are not enough, by themselves, to remove all of our self-loathing and convince our subconscious mind that we are worthy of prosperity and success.

For our subconscious mind to fully believe that we are deserving of reward, such that it aggressively works with our conscious mind rather than against it, it must believe we have not just esteemed ourselves by right-minded thoughts and actions, but that we have forgiven ourselves as well for all the things that have fueled our guilt, shame, self-condemnation and self-loathing.

Unfortunately, no amount of logic, meditation, positive affirmation or therapeutic insight will accomplish this. The only way to truly forgive ourselves is to forgive others.

Here's how it works: When we judge people, we believe our judgments are related to who we think they are or what we think they've done. On one level, there is truth to this. On a deeper, unconscious level, however, our judgments of others have nothing to do with what we think of them, but are actually re-lated to what we think of ourselves.

This process is called projection. It is an unconscious defense mechanism that enables us to avoid experiencing our own guilt by seeing other people as the guilty ones.

> # Projection is a form of unconscious denial.

By projecting onto others what we don't like about ourselves and see-ing them as having negative qualities, not us, we end up feeling good about ourselves, despite having done nothing to eliminate the guilt, shame and self-loathing that is embedded in our unconscious mind.

It's all still there. We haven't gotten rid of it. We've just swept it under the rug, so to speak. Out of sight, out of mind, so to speak.

FORGIVENESS IS THE KEY TO SUCCESS!

Fortunately, we can use this same mechanism of projection to our advantage. If we are projecting our own guilt and self-loathing onto others when we see them in a negative light and judge them harshly, then when we choose to stop seeing them in a negative light, to stop judging them harshly, and to accept and forgive them, we are actually doing the same thing to ourselves. We are actually overlooking our own flaws, accepting ourselves, and forgiving ourselves.

It's as simple as that. Because of the way projection works, when we forgive others, we are forgiving ourselves. As we do this, as we consistently and repeatedly forgive ourselves by forgiving others, our self-esteem increases, our self-loathing decreases, and our self-sabotaging behaviors decrease as well. With this comes accomplishment, self-actualization and success.

As was the case with estimable acts of kindness, when we forgive others it's best that we do it unconditionally and without exceptions or expectations.

If we exclude certain people from our forgiveness, if we decide that some things are forgivable and other things are not, if we place conditions on our forgiveness, or if we expect something from others in return, our subconscious mind will neutralize our efforts to forgive ourselves and will maintain its self-sabotaging stance.

CHAPTER 4

THE PROCESS OF FORGIVENESS

Forgiving others is easier said than done. Our harsh judgments are buried deep within us. They are the root cause of our self-loathing. Our subconscious mind, believing we are loathsome and unworthy, will focus its power on sabotaging our conscious efforts to forgive others by encouraging us to maintain our grievances and resentments. It will persistently tell us that our reasons for not forgiving others are justified and appropriate.

They are not justified and appropriate. There are no good reasons not to forgive others because, regardless of how others have behaved, if we don't forgive them, we're only hurting ourselves. We're only perpetuating our own suffering.

We think we're punishing others when we withhold forgiveness. We think we're beating them up with guilt and shame. However, the ironic truth is that, because of the nature of projection, it is ourselves we're attacking. It is ourselves we're punishing. It is ourselves we're keeping in an emotional prison.

The only way to put an end to this self-punishment is to stop punishing others with our harsh judgments and to forgive them instead.

Consequently, every day we remind ourselves that we are determined to forgive others for our own good. Every day, we remind ourselves that we are determined to forgive others for our own self-esteem and success. Every day we remind ourselves that we are determined to forgive others because not to do so may be gratifying to our petty, selfish, frightened ego, but will forever keep us from the life we want.

FORGIVE AND FORGET

We tell people all the time that we have forgiven them, but the truth is, in most cases, we haven't really done so. If we say we've forgiven people but we harbor any resentment, any thought of how badly they treated us, then we are hanging onto a harsh judgment about them, we are bringing the past into the present, we are reinvesting in our victimhood, and, therefore, we have not truly forgiven them.

Forgiveness and judgment are mutually exclusive. We must always strive to remember this. It doesn't matter if we don't show our judgments. It doesn't matter if we act all lovey-dovey, warm and fuzzy, and the other person has no conscious clue that we are still harboring resentments and hurt from their past actions.

If the resentments are in our mind, we are attacking them with our judgmental thoughts, we are withholding unconditional forgiveness from them, and we will get nowhere. We will still be fanning the flames of guilt, shame, self-condemnation and self-loathing within ourselves, and we will still be sabotaging our efforts to succeed.

We truly must forgive and forget. It's not necessary to literally forget the entire incident that occurred, although that's the ideal scenario which is possible to do.

What is necessary is to release the emotional charge attached to the memory of having been attacked and injured, and to look back at the incident dispassionately (as if we were a third party observer), without any residual judgments and resentments.

Many of us are reluctant to forgive and forget because we believe that, if we forget, we will be placing ourselves in a vulnerable position of getting hurt again. We think that, by hanging onto our memory of past assaults and by judging specific people as possible enemies, we are watching out for ourselves. Ironically, we are subverting ourselves by doing this.

Contrary to the popular belief that "Those who forget the past are doomed to repeat it, the truth is that those who don't forget the past are doomed to repeat it, in the sense that when we don't forget the past, we are re-living it over and over again in our mind, in our present moments, distracting us from being in the Now, reinforcing our beliefs in our victimhood, and reinforcing our unforgiveness.

Truth be told, we can forget past offenses and still be vigilant. We can still be watching out for danger, difficulties and all sorts of bad behaviors by others. We simply do it on a general level, rather than on a specific level.

What this means is: We pay attention to our surroundings so as not to get hurt by others. We keep our radar finely-tuned to alert us to possible threats. We observe details. We watch for red flags and warning signs.

What we don't do is keep a list of specific people to watch out for who have offended us in some way in the past, because, by doing so, we are hanging onto judgments about them and we are placing conditions on our forgiveness.

In essence, we are saying: "I will forgive you, with the condition that I will continue to judge you as a potential threat and watch you closely because you can't truly be trusted not to hurt me again."

Since we have already said that there can be no conditions placed upon forgiveness for us to experience the transformational power of forgiveness, by our keeping a list of past offenders to watch our for, we are placing conditions on our forgiveness and defeating ourselves in the process.

> "We forgive others for our own peace of mind."
> - A Course In Miracles

When we don't forgive others, we're the ones ruminating over what was done to us. We're the ones angry and upset, depressed and anxious. We're the ones getting sick, losing weight and losing sleep, not them.

When we don't forgive others, we're prolonging our own misery and victimizing ourselves long after having been victimized by our offenders.

When we don't forgive others, we relegate ourselves to living in the past, seeing everything through the eyes of the past, and never actually being in the present moment, in the Eternal Now, where all the miraculous aspects of life are apparent and abundant.

OUR RELUCTANCE TO FORGIVE

We are oftentimes reluctant to forgive others because we think that, by doing so, we are making the statement that: (1) We're okay with what they did, (2) We're letting them off the hook and not expecting them to be accountable for their actions, (3) We're weak or foolish, or (4) We're inviting further abuse and victimization.

None of these are true. They are all fear thoughts. They are fabrications of our ego mind, designed to sabotage our efforts by encouraging us to withhold forgiveness.

The truth is that we perceive withholding forgiveness as a way for us to punish people for hurting us, but, as has been said, what we're really doing is punishing ourselves in the process.

The truth is that forgiveness is strength, not weakness. Forgiveness doesn't say to people that we are doormats or suckers, or that it's okay to victimize and abuse us again.

The truth is that forgiveness doesn't mean we condone their actions or are suggesting they not be held accountable.

The truth is that forgiveness doesn't mean we have to be friends with the person we're forgiving or that we have to tolerate their presence or behavior.

Forgiveness simply means that we're letting go of our resentments, our judgments, and our need to make others feel guilty for our own peace of mind and for our own ultimate success.

Make no mistake about it: We forgive others not only for their own good, but for ours. We forgive others not only to make them feel better, but to make us feel better. We forgive others not only to let them out of an emotional prison of guilt, shame and self-loathing, but to let ourselves out of that same emotional prison.

We forgive others not only because it's the Godly, spiritual, compassionate, gracious, generous and merciful thing to do, but because it will heal our mind, our body, and our material reality.

We forgive others so that we can win!

If we are determined to end our self-sabotage and succeed, where in the past we have failed, we must silence our ego's voice and its belief in anger and vengeance, and choose unconditional forgiveness instead.

It takes a lot of humility, determination and vigilance over our thoughts, words and actions, but it can be done.

If we are skeptical about this process of forgiving to win, that's fine. We can be skeptical. We can be cynical. What we can't be is lackadaisical. We must put aside our ego and follow direction. We must work the program.

FORGIVE TO WIN!

On a daily basis, we work towards forgiving those who have injured us in the past, forgiving those who injure us in the present, and letting go of our judgments of others, whether they have done something to us or not.

This latter category is the most critical to attend to because the number of people we need to forgive is relatively small, but the number of people we need to stop judging is infinite.

Everyday we are making judgments about multitudes of people. Everyday we are critical and disapproving of the behaviors and attitudes of those around us.

Even the mildest irritation that flashes across our mind triggered by the presence of another is a harsh judgment.

Insofar as every judgment is an attack thought, insofar as every time we attack another we feel bad about it on an unconscious level and it increases our guilt and shame, and insofar as guilt and shame fuel our self-loathing, when we judge others we are essentially attacking ourselves and compounding the self-sabotaging problems we are trying to resolve.

LETTING GO OF JUDGMENTS

Day to day, person to person, moment to moment, our judgmental thoughts must stop. This is not a simple task. We must continuously challenge the belief that we need judgmental thoughts in order to protect ourselves, prevail and prosper in a chaotic, hostile universe. We don't.

Certainly, we need to evaluate situations, look at people's behaviors and decide if we want to cooperate with them or not, but we don't need to judge them. We need to evaluate their behaviors without attacking their personhood. We need to judge the actions, not the actors. This is a critically important distinction that we must learn to make.

This concept of releasing judgments applies not only to the behaviors and actions of others, but also to the judgments we make about their physical attributes.

Examples of this include: "He's too tall." "She's too short." "She's skinny." "He's fat." "He's smart." "She's stupid." "She's a geek." "He's a dork." "He's ugly." "She's homely." "She's got a big nose." "He's got a big butt."

All sorts of critical judgments, observations and put-downs, some more mean-spirited than others, flash through our minds on a daily basis, in terms of what people look like, how they comb their hair, what clothes they wear, what jewelry they adorn themselves with, what body parts they expose, how they laugh, how they chew their food, what knick-knacks they have on their desk, the list goes on and on.

Despite how innocent or harsh these judgments may seem to be, and despite the fact that they're all in our mind, that we're not expressing them to the people involved, none of them are harmless to us.

They are all attack thoughts which satisfy our ego but subvert our <u>Forgive To Win!</u> goals, and, therefore, must be stopped.

So we do the best we can to eliminate labels of any kind, confident that we will navigate our lives successfully without them. We don't judge people based on their appearances. We choose to see spirits, not bodies, deserving of love, respect and forgiveness, despite how they look or behave.

When we have difficulty letting go of judgments and forgiving others, it behooves us to look at situations from as many different angles as we possibly can, and to find ways to humanize rather than demonize others, in order to soften our hearts, let go of our fears, and forgive them.

"A Call For Love"
- A Course In Miracles

Most people are not intentionally malicious or mean-spirited when they say and do things which we perceive as hurtful and unloving. For the most part, they just aren't thinking. They say and do impulsive, thoughtless things that they later regret.

If we choose to keep this in mind and give others the benefit of the doubt, by considering the possibility that they were not out to get us, and that they meant us no harm, despite what they did being inconsiderate or unkind, it makes it easier for us to forgive them.

It's also easier to forgive others if we choose to see their bad behavior not as an attack but as a call for love. Here's an example:

A husband and wife return from a party. The husband, jealous and enraged, accuses his wife of flirting with the neighbor. He screams at her, calls her names, and emotionally abuses her.

Is he doing this because he hates her? Is he doing this because he never wants to see her again? Is he doing this because he wants a divorce? Not at all.

What's driving his attack is his love and desire for her, coupled with his insecurity and fear that she doesn't really love him and might one day abandon him.

Desperate for her love and reassurance, rather than asking for it directly, in an appropriate way, he asks for it by verbally attacking and abusing her.

Unfortunately, abusing and maligning her is not the solution to his problem. It doesn't inspire her to nurture him and reassure him of her love. On the contrary, it makes her angry and it repels her, which is the exact opposite result that he wants from his actions.

He is his own worst enemy.

Here's the point: When people are abusive towards us in some way, if we see their abuse purely as an unloving attack of cruelty and malevolence, we will resist forgiving them.

However, if we can see their bad behavior, regardless of how dysfunctional and disturbed it might be, not as an attack, but as a twisted, distorted, angry call for love, a crying out for compassion, nurturing and reassurance from someone who is feeling unloved and insecure, and doesn't know how to express it appropriately, it will be easier for us to not get angry and defensive, to empathize, to be understanding, and to forgive them instead.

Stop, Look & Listen!

When the aggression and turbulence is thick, and we are caught up in all the drama and negative energy swirling around us, a technique that can help us ground ourselves is to "Stop, look & listen."

What this means is: We STOP participating in the chaos and confusion. We step back. We disengage. We get quiet and calm. We LOOK at what's happening with compassion, not judgment, with objectivity, not emotion, remembering that, regardless of appearances, everything people do is either an expression of love or a call for love. And then we LISTEN to our Higher Self, our Inner Colleague, that voice we are now cultivating, which will remind us to act appropriately by responding with love, acceptance and forgiveness rather than judgment, resentment and rage.

As has been said, forgiving others is not a simple or easy process. We will resist, despite knowing that it's not in our best interests to do so. Consequently, when we have difficulty forgiving others, we remind ourselves that when we said and did thoughtless, selfish, inconsiderate and unloving things to others in the past, we wished them to understand that we meant no harm and to forgive us, in which case it behooves us to forgive them when the shoe is on the other foot.

A corollary of this is to remind ourselves that regardless of how far we may have spiritually grown and matured, we weren't always where we are now and it was helpful to have others support, encourage, nurture, tolerate, accept and forgive us, rather than assault us with blame, shame and guilt.

GRATITUDE

When we are having difficulty forgiving others, we focus on our blessings and on being grateful for what we have in our lives despite what has been done to us. This can take the sting out of any offense and make it easier for us to let go of our resentments in order to forgive.

When we are having difficulty forgiving others, we remind ourselves that "but for the grace of God go I," that under other, less fortunate circumstances, we might have found ourselves in desperate situations doing unworthy and unloving things to others, out of fear and a belief that they were necessary for our survival.

With humility, we remind ourselves that stressful circumstances can make fools and devils of us all, such that good people do bad things, and, therefore, that it's best to put our harsh judge's robe in the closet and don a cloak of graciousness, compassion and mercy instead.

> # As we sow forgiveness, we reap success.

When we try to walk in another man's shoes, to get a sense of the difficulties he's endured, how he's been damaged in his life, and how he's been programmed from childhood experiences to take and not give, to attack and not love, and to withhold and not share, it provides us with the opportunity to see the offender in a more compassionate light, which then enables us to turn down the intensity of our anger over what has been done to us, to be more empathetic, and to apply the principles of forgiveness.

For example, if we know someone was abused as a child, that can make it easier for us to understand their bad behavior and forgive it. Along the same lines, if we're aware of the current circumstances in the offender's life, such as being unemployed, having no savings, about to be evicted, with a wife and two children to care for, that can make it easier for us to understand why they behaved badly, and to forgive them.

Again: It doesn't mean we're condoning or excusing their behavior, or suggesting they not take responsibility for their bad actions. It just means that we're choosing to see them from a more sympathetic viewpoint, and to let go of our critical judgments.

It can help us to forgive others if we perceive offenders as part of God, despite their ungodly behaviors. Martin Luther King, Jr., once said, "We love men not because we like them or because their ways appeal to us or even because they possess some type of divine spark; we love every man because God loves him."

If we don't believe in God, we use other labels and tools to see the humanity in people despite the errors of their ways.

It's easier to forgive others if we can find some meaning, some wisdom, some benefit born of the assault and the suffering we experienced. If we can do this, if we can find a way to learn and grow from what has happened to us, if we can discover a blessing in disguise, our perspective changes, we feel less angry, less victimized and damaged, and it gives us permission, so to speak, to not resist extending our compassion and forgiveness.

Anger Hurts, Forgiveness Heals

When we find it difficult to forgive others because our anger is so all-consuming and we feel incapable of releasing it, it will help us to remind ourselves that anger is our enemy.

Although anger has value as a signal device for survival, to alert us of danger so we can respond appropriately, most of us hang onto our anger long after it has served its purpose, using it, instead, to assault and manipulate those who have hurt us.

Unfortunately, when we do this, we are hurting ourselves more than anyone else in the process.

Anger deprives us of inner peace and joy. Anger diminishes our capacity to give and receive love. Anger is hazardous to our health.

Anger stimulates the release of stress chemicals that wear down our bodies. Anger raises blood pressure and increases our risk of heart attacks and strokes. Anger depresses our immune system, makes us more vulnerable to diseases and cancer, and makes it more difficult for us to recover from illnesses and injuries.

Anger causes us to be emotionally imbalanced, sometimes to the point of making very impulsive, irrational, reckless decisions that have dire physical consequences for ourselves and others.

Insofar as forgiveness decreases our anger and heals us emotionally and physically, it's a no-brainer that the smart money is on forgiveness, and that to stay angry at others is the real sucker play.

There is absolutely no advantage to staying angry. If we understand the danger our anger alerted us to, we'll know what to watch out for in the future for our safety and security, and it won't be necessary to hang onto our anger.

Eventually, we'll understand that we can take care of ourselves and protect our interests just as well, if not better, when we are calm and non-reactive.

Rise Above The Battlefield

We have been trained to believe in concepts like "survival of the fittest" and "every man for himself," which suggests that we must battle others if we are to succeed and prevail.

This sort of philosophy makes it difficult to release judgment and attack thoughts, because it serves to fuel our animosity and aggression, which we believe we need in order to survive.

The truth is that we do not need animosity and aggression in order to survive. The truth is that we will not prevail, in the long run, as long as we believe we must attack and destroy others in order to do so.

Therefore, it behooves us to find a way to rise above the battlefield, to perceive the world in a different light, so that we can appreciate the foolishness of attacking others and withholding forgiveness.

One way to do this is to consider the analogy of a jigsaw puzzle. Each jigsaw puzzle piece looks different in some way from other pieces, but each piece is inherently the same, in the sense that each piece is an integral part of the puzzle that contributes to the puzzle's wholeness. Without every single piece, the puzzle is not complete.

It would be irrational and self-destructive for one puzzle piece to hurt or destroy another puzzle piece, because the integrity of the whole puzzle, which each piece is ultimately dependent upon, would be damaged in the process.

Applying this analogy to human beings and God: If God is the jigsaw puzzle and human beings are pieces of that puzzle, then when we attack one another, we are being irrational and self-destructive, because we are attacking the integrity of God, who we are all dependent upon for our ultimate, long-term survival.

The same analogy holds up if we replace God with Mother Nature, the Universal Mind, or some other label. However we define the Oneness of Life, it behooves us to "love ye one another."

When we have difficulty doing this, it might help to consider the Biblical quote, "The meek shall inherit the earth." Perhaps this doesn't mean those who are weak and submissive, but rather those who are humble, accepting and forgiving.

CHAPTER 5

THE FORGIVENESS DIET

It's all well and good to know what we need to do. It's nice to have tools to help us deal with our resistance to engaging in estimable acts and forgiving others. But if we now have to go forth and implement these behaviors without structure and augmentation strategies, it is unlikely that we will establish habits that will endure and deliver us the results we desire.

That is the basis for having created the Forgiveness Diet, a structured regimen of daily routines and exercises to help us establish and maintain our focus and commitment to estimable acts of kindness and forgiveness.

As we practice the Forgiveness Diet on a daily basis, as rigorously as possible, without placing conditions on our choices and actions, and without making exceptions for particular people or situations, we begin to repair the embedded, negative self-definitions which have been holding us back.

In so doing, our subconscious mind gets the message that we are worthy of reward instead of punishment, and starts empowering us in all realms material, physical, emotional and spiritual, instead of sabotaging us as it has done in the past.

Over time, we see our lives working better. We see progress being made towards long-range goals that have forever seemed elusive.

A SPIRITUAL FOOD PLAN

The Forgiveness Diet has been broken down into components that parallel a diet one might initiate in order to lose weight. This was done for the sake of making analogies that are easy to understand, and to provide an easy way to utilize rating scales to document our progress.

The requirements of the Forgiveness Diet include: (1) A high intake of spiritual protein, (2) A low intake of spiritual fat, (3) A low intake of spiritual sugar, (4) A high intake of spiritual fiber, (5) A monitoring of spiritual calories, (6) A high intake of spiritual water, (7) Spiritual supplements, (8) Spiritual exercises, and (9) Spiritual scales to measure the effectiveness of the Forgiveness Diet and the increase in our material success.

HIGH INTAKE OF SPIRITUAL PROTEIN

The spiritual proteins of the Forgiveness Diet are the estimable acts of kindness and the giving to others of unconditional forgiveness. Just as proteins are the building blocks of life, estimable acts of kindness and forgiveness are the building blocks that will repair our damaged sense of self and our core self-misperceptions which are responsible for our self-sabotage.

Consequently, every day it is essential that we engage in large quantities of estimable acts as detailed in Chapter 3. Every day we look for opportunities to be of service to others, and to extend consideration, generosity, and selflessness to everyone we encounter. "What can I do to help you?" becomes the prime directive, rather than, "What's in it for me?"

Every day we offer, we share, we care, we go the distance, we go above and beyond, we role model unconditional forgiveness, compassion and right action without need of acknowledgement, thanks or other forms of compensation.

Every day we engage in estimable behaviors, large and small, extending our humanity and generosity to everyone we can, under all circumstances, without exceptions or conditions, and regardless of how they are behaving.

In every way, we offer service to others, regardless of who they are or what they've done in the past. We let bygones be bygones. We forgive and forget.

If our actions and good deeds fall on deaf ears, are unappreciated, ridiculed, misinterpreted, or used in other ways as ammunition against us, we stick to our game plan, we persevere unphased. We turn the other cheek. We forgive them for they know not what they do.

When we forget why we do this, we remind ourselves that it's in our own best interests to do so, that by getting out of the way of our ego and self-doubt, and persisting in the practice of estimable acts of selflessness, we will repair our core identity defects, end our self-loathing, end our self-sabotage, and manifest the destiny we desire.

LOW INTAKE OF SPIRITUAL FAT

Spiritual fat in the Forgiveness Diet is equivalent to judgments and other attack thoughts. Just as fat clogs the physical arteries and contributes to heart attacks, so does spiritual fat clog our spiritual arteries, contribute to our emotional heartache, and block the flow of love and compassion in our lives.

Keeping in mind that what clogs the spiritual arteries and blocks the flow of love and compassion ultimately clogs the "material arteries" and blocks the flow of success and prosperity in our lives, it behooves us, on a daily basis, to put aside our judgments, biases, grievances, jealousies, and resentments towards others.

We embrace and honor diversity while at the same time acknowledging the similarities that we share with others. We cast aside our ego's perceptions of differences and distinctions that divide and separate us, and replace them with unifying principles of tolerance and acceptance that recognize the love and humanity inherent within each of us.

We overlook the flaws and imperfections of others, and always choose to find the common ground.

When we reduce the spiritual fat in our lives by letting go of our judgments and being mindful of the sacredness of every human being, we repair our fragmented self, we heal our spiritual wounds, and we release ourselves from the emotional, physical and material prison we presently find ourselves trapped in.

LOW INTAKE OF SPIRITUAL SUGAR

Spiritual sugar in the Forgiveness Diet refers to things in our lives that provide us with immediate gratification, but are not in our best interests in the long run.

Just as there are foods containing sugar which are fun to eat, but can lead to a variety of health problems down the road, there are behaviors we indulge in that provide us with pleasure in the moment but which are counter-productive and self-destructive.

Some examples include: (1) Playing practical jokes and getting laughs at other people's expense, (2) Being sarcastic and ridiculing people, (3) Flirting inappropriately with people, and (4) Gossiping about people and spreading rumors.

All of these examples are different forms of aggression and psychological assault which we perceive, in the moment, to be amusing, entertaining and pleasurable. Unfortunately, by indulging in the joys of selfish, thoughtless, mean-spirited and unloving ego gratification, whether conscious of it or not, we set the stage for retaliation and other negative repercussions, in addition to reinforcing our subconscious self-loathing, all of which is to say that high levels of spiritual sugar are hazardous to our Forgive To Win! health.

HIGH INTAKE OF SPIRITUAL FIBER

The spiritual fiber of the Forgiveness Diet is equivalent to moral fiber. Just as fiber intake in the physical body assists in a variety of physiological processes and contributes to our overall well-being and longevity, spiritual fiber helps our spiritual body to operate at maximum efficiency, and to insure that we stay focused on our goals and don't veer off our path towards our material success.

A high intake of spiritual fiber is equivalent to high levels of honesty, integrity, ethics, right-mindedness and fair-mindedness in all our transactions. This includes respecting the integrity of animals and nature as well.

And so it behooves us to do the best we can, every day, to tell the truth, to say what we mean, to walk the talk, to practice what we preach, to not distort or misrepresent, to not cheat or defraud people, to not make promises we don't intend to keep, and to not manipulate circumstances to gain unfair advantage and undeserved profits.

Another type of spiritual fiber we need large quantities of on a daily basis involves being honest with ourselves, which means we learn to recognize and, over time, release our defense mechanisms, rather than hide behind them as we've done in the past.

Despite it being true that the Forgiveness Diet does not require us to use therapeutic, insight-oriented techniques for it to work wonders in our lives, it still behooves us to, as best we can, recognize when we are in denial, when we are rationalizing our behavior, and when we are displacing our aggression onto others inappropriately, so that we can stop doing these things, take responsibility for our actions, make wiser, more empowering life choices based on truth and compassion rather than ego and fear, and accelerate the Forgive To Win! process.

MONITORING OF SPIRITUAL CALORIES

The spiritual calories of the Forgiveness Diet are equivalent to spiritual errors, such as, among others, not engaging in estimable acts, not being loving and forgiving, being judgmental and angry, and being oppositional and obstructive.

Just as a regular diet encourages the daily monitoring of calories so as to keep them to a minimum, the Forgiveness Diet encourages a daily monitoring of our spiritual calories, in order to keep them to a minimum as well.

Consequently, at the end of each day, we do a Forgiveness Inventory to assess how successful we were in applying the Forgiveness Diet. We review the day's events, acknowledging our errors, mistakes and transgressions, and examining the ways in which we could have behaved better and been more compassionate.

We ask ourselves: "What did we do that was cruel and contracted, petty, selfish and unloving? Were we resentful, bitter and withholding? Were we ungracious? Were we rude and arrogant? Did we make a joke at someone else's expense? Were we sarcastic, belittling, demeaning and insulting? Were we controlling and manipulative? Did we use our power or position to minimize or take advantage of someone else?"

"Did we cheat? Did we lie? Did we steal? Did we rationalize bad behavior because it helped us look good or get us what we wanted, even though it really wasn't right or fair? Were we thoughtless and inconsiderate? Were we jealous or unnecessarily competitive?"

It is important that we look at each day's missed opportunities and poor or failed attempts, in order for us to learn from our mistakes and make better choices in days to come, in order to accelerate our spiritual and our material progress.

Every evening after doing our Forgiveness Inventory, we make a Forgiveness Inventory List of the things we wish to do the following day, in terms of behaviors we wish to modify or eliminate.

If we were rude to someone, we make a note on the list to be more tolerant and patient. If we were irritable and angry towards someone, we make a note on the list to let go of the resentment and be more compassionate and understanding. If we were inconsiderate and selfish with someone, we make a note on the list to be more thoughtful and generous.

If we hurt others, whether intentionally or not, whether they hurt us first and "deserved" it or not, we put it on the list to apologize, to make amends, to take responsibility for our hurtful choices and actions, regardless of whether or not others take responsibility for theirs.

What others do is not our concern. Getting our own house in order is, which is why every morning we review the previous evening's Forgiveness Inventory List, reminding ourselves of the specific behaviors we wish to discontinue or improve upon, so that our daily actions consistently reflect estimable acts of truth, compassion, acceptance, calmness and forgiveness.

SPIRITUAL WATER

Just as water can facilitate weight loss when we are on a physical diet, spiritual water can increase the effectiveness of the Forgiveness Diet.

Spiritual water in the Forgiveness Diet refers to the use of Forgiveness Mantras, expressions of our truths that we wish to keep in the forefront of our mind in order to keep us focused on our goals and moving forward on our path.

Consequently, every hour or two throughout the day we take a minute to repeat our Forgiveness Mantras silently to ourselves.

Examples of Forgiveness Mantras we can use are: (1) "Anger hurts, forgiveness heals," to remind us, when we are angry, resentful and unwilling to forgive, that withholding forgiveness and hanging onto anger hurts us more than anyone else; (2) "Everything is love or a call for love," to remind us, when we are confronted with someone who is angry, hostile, withholding, unloving, and abusive, that they are actually in deep, emotional pain, and that the best response we can offer is not defensiveness and anger, but rather some form of love, compassion, understanding and validation; and (3) "I see the love in everyone. There is nothing else to see."

We can design our own Forgiveness Mantras and we can choose to repeat them to ourselves as frequently as we'd like. We can print our Forgiveness Mantras on Post-It notes and place them on our desk, our computer, the bathroom mirror, the car dashboard, the refrigerator, and wherever else our eyes might spot them throughout the day.

The more we keep our mind fixed on thoughts that reinforce our goals, the faster we will assimilate the Forgiveness Diet into our daily routines and see the results we desire.

SPIRITUAL SUPPLEMENTS

Just as we add vitamins and herbal supplements to augment our nutrition and improve our physical well-being, we utilize spiritual supplements to augment the effectiveness of our efforts and to improve our spiritual and material well-being.

Our spiritual supplements include Forgiveness Affirmations, Forgiveness Visualizations, a Gratitude List, Synchronistic Contemplations, and Dream Programming.

FORGIVENESS AFFIRMATIONS

Thoughts precede actions. Negative thoughts generate negative actions and positive thoughts generate positive actions. If we want to change our negative actions of withholding, being unforgiving and being unwilling to engage in estimable acts, then we must replace our negative thoughts of judgment and attack with positive thoughts of acceptance and forgiveness.

Forgiveness Affirmations are a way to do this. They are a way to program our subconscious mind to believe what we wish it to believe so it will do our bidding and generate the world we want.

Forgiveness Affirmations do not need to be complicated. They just need to be repeated. Some examples of appropriate Forgiveness Affirmations are: (1) Every day and in every way I esteem and forgive others; (2) Every day and in every way I give up my judgments and attack thoughts; (3) Every day and in every way it becomes easier to forgive and forget; (4) Every day and in every way it becomes easier to engage in estimable acts; (5) Every day and in every way it becomes easier to let go of grievances and resentments; and (6) Every day and in every way I make wise choices that benefit myself and the world.

If we tell ourselves these things repeatedly, fervently, with intense passion and conviction, as if there is no question that what we're saying is the absolute truth, we are increasing the potential for our subconscious mind to manifest a reality that conforms to these ideas and paves the way for success and prosperity.

FORGIVENESS VISUALIZATIONS

Visualizations are another way of programming our subconscious mind to do our bidding. With visualizations, the imprinting is done with images rather than words. Forgiveness Visualizations are particularly helpful when we're having difficulty forgiving others.

We begin a visualization exercise by first getting into a comfortable position at a time when we won't be distracted or disturbed, closing our eyes, and then relaxing our entire body.

When we feel sufficiently relaxed, we begin the Forgiveness Visualization: First, we visualize ourselves walking alone along a desolate road in the dead of night. It is dark, windy, and cold.

There is a light in the distance. We walk toward the light. As we get closer we see a bridge. On the other side of the bridge is a beautiful garden brightly lit, emanating serenity and love.

As we approach the bridge we see our offender, a person who we are having trouble forgiving, attempting to cross the bridge to the garden. The bridge consists of rotted wooden planks wrapped in thorns and barbed wire. He/she is unable to make any headway.

It quickly becomes apparent that the only way anyone can cross the bridge and enter the garden is with the help of another. It cannot be done alone.

We reluctantly grab the hand of our offender and together we stabilize each other as we navigate a path across the bridge.

Focusing all our energy on cooperation and survival, our anger, our hurt, our resentments, our grievances, our harsh judgments, and our fantasies of retaliation and retribution towards our offender leave our mind.

When we arrive on the other side of the bridge at the entrance to the garden, we look at our offender, who has just helped us get across the Forgiveness Bridge to the Garden of Serenity, Light and Love, with a deep sense of compassion, forgiveness, and gratitude, knowing that we could never have gotten there on our own without his help.

The more we use this Forgiveness Visualization with those we are having trouble forgiving, the more we will observe a decrease in our anger and reactivity along with an increase in our capacity to let go of resentments, accept the limitations of others, and forgive them.

A GRATITUDE LIST

A Gratitude List is an extremely helpful augmentation strategy. When we feel deprived, lacking, unloved, and limited, it oftentimes tends to make us more contracted, more resentful, more envious, and more jealous of others.

It puts us in a mode of comparison and competition, where we begrudge what others have and we resent their good fortune. We become preoccupied with the thought, "Why should I help you when I don't have what I want?"

This leads to us being withholding, unwilling to help others, and not wanting to give or to share.

Conversely, when we count our blessings, despite the lack and limitations in our lives, when we acknowledge the good things we have, despite what we don't have, when we appreciate that a lot of people have it a whole lot worse than we do, and when we are grateful for the things that are going right in our lives, despite what's going wrong, it makes it easier for us to be more gracious and understanding.

It makes it easier for us to engage in estimable acts and to extend kindnesses and blessings to others. It makes it easier for us to be less judgmental, more tolerant, more accepting, and more forgiving.

Consequently, we create a personal Gratitude List, which reflects all the positive things in our lives that we have to be grateful for, and we review the list on a daily basis, so that, when an opportunity to be kind and generous arises, we will be more inclined to share what we've got and to help in whatever way we can, furthering our own <u>Forgive To Win!</u> goals in the process.

SYNCHRONISTIC CONTEMPLATIONS

Synchronistic Contemplations are a way to utilize the Collective Unconscious which has two important principles: (1) All minds are connected to each other at an unconscious level, and (2) The Collective Unconscious receives all the unconscious needs of individual minds prior to events being manifested in physical reality, and then organizes and synchronizes people and circumstances, at an unconscious level, such that people come together at the appropriate time and in the appropriate place for everyone's unconscious needs to be met.

Think of the Collective Unconscious as a cosmic Craig's List, where people who want to get something are connected with people who have something to give. For example, if we want to rent an apartment, and somebody has an apartment they want to rent, the Collective Unconscious engineers circumstances so that we are directed to the appropriate party and everybody wins.

This is, essentially, the mechanism of the Law of Attraction: What we want at an unconscious level we attract to us. When we like ourselves there will be no resistance to the flow of positive energy and we will attract people and circumstances that favor us because our subconscious mind will be working with us rather than against us to manifest ideal outcomes in our lives.

Conversely, when we don't like ourselves, and our unconscious desire is to be punished because of it, our subconscious mind will sabotage us such that we do not connect with the right people, we are not at the right place at the right time, we attract negative and unsavory elements into our world, and we are victimized.

When we look at reality formation in this way, we can appreciate the importance of sufficiently esteeming ourselves so that the Collective Unconscious engineers the attraction of empowering people and circumstances without obstacles and resistance.

We can also appreciate the importance of paying attention to synchronistic signs generated by the Collective Unconscious as it is engineering our physical reality.

A synchronistic sign is a meaningful coincidence: two or more events occurring simultaneously that seem to be unrelated but are actually connected at a level our conscious mind cannot discern. Its purpose is reality emphasis, the universe using the juxtaposition of two seemingly unrelated events to get our attention and point us in a specific direction.

If we are perceptive, we may recognize synchronistic signs, not write them off as meaningless coincidences, and interpret them in ways that guide us along the path of least resistance to the most effective actualization of our goals. This is the basis for our doing Synchronistic Contemplations.

Here's how it works: When we look back at incidents in our day that are unusual and coincidental (such as altering our normal routine for some reason and then bumping into someone we haven't seen in months or years, or thinking about what to do over the weekend and then, moments later, getting a phone call inviting us to an event on Saturday night), it behooves us to pay attention, to not take those people or those invitations too lightly, but rather to consider the possibility that they may be signposts on our life path encouraging us to go in one direction versus another, and to also consider the possibility that no one is sent to us by accident.

A word of advice: It would be a mistake to assume that every synchronistic signpost is in our best interests and should be followed. Some of the signposts we encounter might be generated by our unconscious desire to sabotage ourselves and designed to lead us down the wrong path. We, therefore, must contemplate the potentials of every event that we encounter in order to take advantage of opportunities as well as to avoid obstacles and setbacks.

Initially, this will be a difficult process, but as we do it repeatedly, we become better at identifying and interpreting the synchronistic signs, and navigating our life path more effectively.

DREAM PROGRAMMING

If we are having problems engaging in estimable acts of kindness and in forgiving others, despite knowing it's in our best interests in the long run to do so, we can ask for help in our dreams.

Prior to going to sleep, we tell ourselves that in our dreams we will work through our conflicts and our fears which are holding us back in our waking life. We tell ourselves that in our dreams we will work on our resistance to being of service, giving, and forgiving.

If we are having trouble with giving to or forgiving specific people, we tell ourselves that in our dreams we will give to, esteem and forgive those people in particular.

If we program our dreams in these ways, it will have an impact on our dream life and increase our potential to give and forgive in our waking life.

And we can go one step further:

LUCID DREAMING

In a normal dream, we are not aware that we are dreaming. We think what is happening is real and that we have no control over the dream reality.

In a lucid dream, we become aware of the fact that we are dreaming and that what we are viewing is the dream landscape and not physical reality.

When we experience a lucid dream, when we essentially are awake in our dream, we can initiate changes in the dream world with our thoughts and direct the outcome of the dream.

We can tell ourselves, while in the lucid dream state, that we want to talk to a particular person or go to a particular place, and it will instantly happen. If we find ourselves face to face with someone who, for example, we're having trouble forgiving, we can forgive them in our lucid dream and it will have an impact on our waking life.

This is because when we overcome a problem in a lucid dream, we are telling our subconscious mind that we have resolved the problem. Our subconscious mind (believing what it is told) now believes we have healed, to some degree, our guilt, shame and self-loathing, in which case it is less inclined to sabotage us.

Lucid dreams happen spontaneously, such that we suddenly become aware that we're in a dream and that what we think is reality isn't real.

We can also make lucid dreams happen. For example, if we're dreaming that we're talking to our high school biology teacher and we realize that this makes no sense because he died several years ago, this cognitive dissonance can make us realize that we must be dreaming.

At this point, we are awake in our dream. We are lucid dreaming. We are viewing the dreamscape. We can now direct the dream with our conscious thoughts.

Consequently, it behooves us at night, when we're programming our dreams before going to sleep, to ask ourselves for a lucid dream experience and to tell ourselves who we want to talk to and forgive should a lucid dream happen.

Whether we have lucid dreams or not, the process of programming our dreams with requests to esteem and forgive others has the potential to heal our mind and alter the agenda of our subconscious in favor of supporting our goals and aspirations, rather than subverting them.

SPIRITUAL EXERCISE

Just as physical exercise is of value in a diet to help us lose physical weight, spiritual exercise is valuable in a spiritual diet to help us lose our spiritual weight, to help us enlighten ourselves.

Spiritual exercise in the Forgiveness Diet consists of Mindfulness Calisthenics. Each morning we spend a few minutes engaging in some form of physical exercise that will get our blood flowing and energize our body, such as jumping jacks, jogging around the living room, or dancing.

While we are doing this, we repeat our Mindfulness Reminders to ourselves, in order to energize our mind as well as our body for the upcoming day. Some examples of Mindfulness Reminders include: I'm happy. I'm loving. I'm lovable. I love helping people. I love forgiving people. I'm deserving of abundance and success.

SPIRITUAL SCALES

With regular diets, we use scales to weigh ourselves and monitor our progress. With the Forgiveness Diet, there are three Self-Rating Scales that we use to spiritually weigh ourselves, monitor our material progress and uncover areas requiring greater attention.

The three Self-Rating Scales are: (1) the Self-Sabotaging Scale, (2) the Self-Actualization Scale, and (3) the Forgiveness Diet Success Scale.

The Self-Sabotaging Scale reveals to what degree we are conquering versus continuing to indulge our self-defeating behaviors. The Self-Actualization Scale reveals to what degree we are satisfied with what we have accomplished in material areas of our lives. The Forgiveness Diet Success Scale reveals to what degree we are following the Forgiveness Diet's Spiritual Food Plan.

As we use these scales over time to monitor our program, we will see a very clear correlation between the three scales. As our Forgiveness Diet Success scores increase, our Self-Sabotaging scores will decrease and our Self-Actualization scores will increase.

In other words, over time, we'll see that the Forgiveness Diet works.

Samples of the three Self-Rating Scales and instructions on how to use them can be found in the Appendix.

GETTING STARTED

Each morning when we wake up, we spend five minutes doing our Mindfulness Calisthenics and our Mindfulness Reminders.

Then we take five minutes to lie down, calm our mind, review our Gratitude List and review our Forgiveness Inventory List, which focuses on what areas we need to pay particular attention to during the upcoming day.

During the day, we engage in estimable acts, we forgive others, and we repeat our Forgiveness Mantras approximately every 1-2 hours.

Each evening, we spend fifteen minutes working on our Forgiveness Inventory, creating our Forgiveness Inventory List for the following day, and engaging in our Synchronistic Contemplations.

Before going to sleep, we spend fifteen minutes doing our Forgiveness Affirmations, our Forgiveness Visualizations, and our Dream Programming.

A WORD TO THE WISE

As we engage in the Forgiveness Diet, family members, friends, co-workers, and/or neighbors (because of their own fear, insecurity and self-loathing) will, consciously or unconsciously, try to make us feel stupid and foolish for doing so.

Threatened by our efforts to create a new life for ourselves, they may tease and ridicule us for being "too nice." They may tell us we're being doormats, suckers, and chumps, and that we're being taken advantage of by people who don't deserve our kind acts, forgiveness and compassion.

When they do this, it is not out of maliciousness, but rather due to two likely scenarios: (1) They are afraid that if we change ourselves and our lives, we will abandon them for greener pastures, and/or (2) They are threatened by our efforts to improve ourselves, which make them uncomfortable with the fact that they are doing nothing to improve themselves. If they can influence us to go back to doing nothing, it will make them feel better about themselves doing nothing.

The best thing to do in these circumstances is to: (1) Reassure them of our love and commitment to them, (2) Encourage them to make similar changes in their lives, and (3) Request that, regardless of their fears and their feelings, they be positive and supportive of us during this new life approach we're undertaking.

ROME WASN'T BUILT IN A DAY

What we're attempting to do is the most difficult assignment we have ever given ourselves. It's by no means a simple process to change deeply-engrained thoughts, emotions, and behaviors. It will take time.

It is unrealistic to anticipate the kind of change, growth, success and prosperity we're talking about here happening overnight. It is wiser to expect gradual improvements in our lives.

Periodically, our ego will shout at us that, "It's taking too long, it's not going to work, give it up!" But we don't listen. We don't veer from our path. We stay the course. We do the best that we can.

When we find ourselves getting impatient, frustrated and discouraged because results aren't happening fast enough, we remind ourselves that utilizing a tool which will dramatically transform the lives and realities of ourselves and all those we touch requires time for the synchronization of cooperating people and circumstances.

We remind ourselves of the story about the tortoise and the hare: that slow and steady progress wins the race.

More than anything else, we remind ourselves that the patience required of us in the daily application of the Forgiveness Diet is patience that will pay off, compared to all of our time, money and efforts in the past which have not.

TWO STEPS FORWARD, ONE STEP BACK

In addition to acknowledging the importance of patience, we must also acknowledge that there will be good days and bad days, and that we shouldn't allow the bad days to set us back or derail us either.

Good days and bad days are part of the normal progression of change and growth. Two steps forward, one step back. That's how it works. No point in getting frustrated by it or giving it more power than it deserves.

When we have our bad days, when we find ourselves slipping back into our old habits and counterproductive behavior patterns, we don't beat ourselves up with guilt, shame, and self-condemnation.

We just get back to applying and practicing the Forgiveness Diet, one day at a time, one moment at a time, one choice at a time. We don't dwell on how long it took us to get going again. We don't deride and degrade ourselves for getting derailed in the first place. We just get back to the program.

We just get back to rigorously practicing the Forgiveness Diet on a daily basis, knowing that it is the surest way to forgive ourselves, end our self-sabotage, and harness the inherent power within us, in order to self-actualize the fullness of our potential.

> # Be the Light.
> # End self-sabotage.
> # You can have it all!

CHAPTER 6

GETTING EVERYTHING YOU WANT!

If we practice the Forgiveness Diet diligently, earnestly and honestly every day, it will be a life-transforming experience that can't help but make our lives better.

Over time, we will see tangible, unequivocal evidence of less self-sabotage, less resistance, less bad luck and fewer missed opportunities.

We will see ourselves making better choices, attracting healthier people and circumstances, and manifesting greater blessings in all realms of our lives.

THE SUCCESS DIET

It's at this point that, if we did nothing more than continue to practice and apply the principles of the Forgiveness Diet on a daily basis, we would continue to see benefits and improvements manifesting in our lives.

However, to optimize our opportunities and accelerate the process of manifesting success and abundance, when the Forgiveness Diet becomes a well-established habit, we have the option of introducing a Success Diet into our daily routine, which is similar in form to the Forgiveness Diet but differs in content, in that it specifically focuses on our life goals and ambitions.

The first step in implementing a Success Diet is to clearly define what our life goals actually are, in terms of our health, our relationships, our career and our finances. We ask ourselves where we'd like to see ourselves in five years, what we'd like to have accomplished, and what we'd like to have acquired in the material world.

The next step is to clearly define specific efforts we need to initiate in order to move us in the direction of the goals we've outlined.

The final step is to integrate these specific efforts into our already-established, daily Forgiveness Diet routine. Here's how it works:

Each morning, we utilize Mindfulness Success Reminders while doing our Mindfulness Calisthenics. Some examples of Mindfulness Success Reminders include: I'm successful. I'm prosperous. I'm resourceful. I'm proactive. I'm energized. I'm inspired. I'm confident. I'm assertive. I'm effective.

Next we review our Gratitude List and our Success Inventory List, which tells us what we need to focus on and implement that day to move us forward on our success path.

During the day, we are proactive. We network. We engage. We follow through. And we repeat our Success Mantras to ourselves throughout the day to keep us focused on the truth. Examples of Success Mantras include: (1) I am not a victim of the world I see. I am the master of my fate; (2) My thoughts create my reality; and (3) I give no power to fear.

Every evening, we do our Success Inventory, evaluating the effectiveness of our efforts during that day, and we generate a new Success Inventory List to guide the following day's activities.

Some of the questions we ask ourselves while doing our Success Inventory include: What did I do that was proactive and positive? What did I do that was sabotaging and self-destructive? What could I have done differently? Did I recognize and take advantage of opportunities? Did I communicate effectively? Did I follow up on loose ends? Did I fulfill my commitments?

We also engage in Synchronistic Contemplations to help guide our choices.

Before bedtime, we do our Success Affirmations and Success Visualizations, and we program our dreams in order to resolve roadblocks and provide us with innovative solutions.

Some examples of Success Affirmations include: (1) Every day and in every way I am becoming more successful and prosperous; (2) Every day and in every way I increase my efficiency and productivity; (3) Every day and in every way I inspire cooperation and assistance from others; (4) Every day and in every way I strengthen and expand my network; (5) Every day and in every way I make wiser choices; and (6) Every day and in every way I generate good will and maximize my opportunities.

Here's an example of a Success Visualization: After getting into a comfortable position and relaxing ourselves at a time and in a place where we won't be distracted or interrupted, we visualize ourselves having already accomplished our goals and living the life we desire. We visualize as much detail as possible and we fill our mind with the joy of accomplishment and success.

PATIENCE IS A VIRTUE

It is critical that we not seek shortcuts. If we introduce our Success Diet before the Forgiveness Diet has been firmly embedded in our psyche and firmly established as a daily habit in our lives, we will be sabotaging the Forgive To Win! formula.

Consequently, after 90 days of engaging in the Forgiveness Diet, if it has not become a way of life as automatic as brushing our teeth in the morning, we do not start the Success Diet.

We remain patient, calm, positive and optimistic. We persist and persevere. We keep working the Forgiveness Diet program until we have it down pat.

Then, when we integrate our Success Diet into our Forgiveness Diet routines, we will be maximizing the materialization of our dreams without resistance or negative consequences of any kind, thereby increasing the odds in our favor of getting the success that we desire.

APPENDIX

RATING SCALES

Before beginning our 90-Day <u>Forgive To Win!</u> program, we do our Spiritual Scales to get a starting baseline of where we are at. Thereafter, we repeat the Spiritual Scales at the end of 30, 60 and 90 days in order to assess our progress.

SELF-SABOTAGING SCALE

Below is a list of general Self-Sabotaging behaviors. The list can be modified so as to best reflect our own specific self-sabotaging behaviors we want to monitor and work on. We rate each item on a scale of 1 to 10, where 1 is the least severe and 10 is the most severe.

At the end of each month we can compare the ratings, see the progress we're making, and what areas we need to focus on.

SELF-SABOTAGING BEHAVIORS

Procrastinating
Not Completing Projects
Not Fulfilling Promises & Obligations
Not Showing Up / Showing Up Late

Not Returning Calls / Returning Calls Late
Eating, Drinking, Drugging Too Much
Sleeping Too Much / Not Sleeping Enough
Not Exercising Enough
Partying Too Much
Spending Too Much
Gambling Too Much
TV, Computer, Videogames Too Much
Isolating & Avoiding Too Much
Being Oppositional Too Much
Being Judgmental Too Much
Expressing Anger & Aggression Too Much
Expressing Passive-Aggression Too Much
Contempt Prior To Investigation Too Much

SELF-ACTUALIZATION SCALE

Below is a list of Self-Actualization Goals. The list can be modified so as to best reflect our own specific self-actualization goals we want to monitor. We rate each item on a scale of 1 to 10, where 1 reflects minimal actualization of the goal and 10 reflects maximum actualization of the goal.

At the end of each month we can compare the ratings, see the progress we're making, and what areas we need to focus on.

SELF-ACTUALIZATION GOALS

Money
Home Ownership
Savings & Investments

Career Advancement
Love Relationships
Friendship Relationships
Health Maintenance & Longevity
Dieting & Weight Loss
Exercise & Bodybuilding
Religious / Spiritual
Personal Power & Confidence
Happiness
Inner Peace

FORGIVENESS DIET SUCCESS SCALE

Below is a list of the Forgiveness Diet Spiritual Food Plan Components. We rate each item on a scale of 1 to 10, where 1 reflects minimal compliance with the Component and 10 reflects maximum compliance with the Component.

At the end of each month we can compare the ratings, see the progress we're making, and what areas we need to focus on.

FORGIVENESS DIET COMPONENTS

High Intake of Spiritual Protein (Estimable Acts & Forgiveness)
Low Intake of Spiritual Fat (Judgments & Resentments)
Low Intake of Spiritual Sugar (Immediate Ego Gratification)
High Intake of Spiritual Fiber (Truth, Morality & Ethics)
Monitoring of Spiritual Calories (Forgiveness Inventory & List)
High Intake of Spiritual Water (Forgiveness Mantras)
High Intake of Spiritual Supplements

Forgiveness Affirmations
Forgiveness Visualizations
Gratitude List
Synchronistic Contemplations
Dream Programming
High Intake of Spiritual Exercise (Mindfulness Calisthenics &
Mindfulness Reminders)

Made in the USA
Charleston, SC
17 November 2011